TORKOM SARAYDARIAN

OLYMPUS

World Report...The Year 3000

T.S.G.
PUBLISHING FOUNDATION

Visions for the Twenty-First Century®

Olympus World Report...The Year 3000

©1993 The Creative Trust

ISBN: 0-929874-46-3

Library of Congress Catalog Card Number: 92-85571

Printed in the United States of America

Cover Design: *Fine Point Graphics*
                       Sedona, Arizona

Printed by: *Data Repoductions Corp.*
                       Rochester Hills, Michigan

Published by: **T.S.G. Publishing Foundation**, Inc.

T.S.G. Publishing Foundation, Inc.
Visions for the 21st Century®
P.O. Box 7068
Cave Creek, AZ 85331-7068 U.S.A.

Table of Contents

...We are sufficiently aware that perfection is attained not through dwelling in the past, but by unrestrainable striving into the future. We advise, especially now, to transport your entire consciousness into the future, thus avoiding many fetters of past existences.

Heart, para. 152

The future of humanity, the future of the Cosmos — is there anything more sacred?

New Era Community, para. 199

Forecasts for the Future

The following forecasts for the next millinium are not the products of a psychic, medium, or channel. These forecasts have been compiled along scientific lines in an attempt to discover what will really occur in the future based on what we scientifically observe, know, and see in the present. They have also been compiled following extensive research of esoteric literature.

According to the Teaching, a great future awaits humanity. The "Captain" of the "ship" is alert and able, and conditions will gradually improve. Though many are suffering and will continue to suffer, the future of humanity is bright.

The first forecast is for the year 2025. Due to an increasing desire for international understanding, cooperation, and unity, all military installations will start collapsing by that year. In the next five to six years, we will witness how average humanity will become more unified and understanding, exerting tremendous pressure upon world leadership to bring humanity into synthesis. The result will be that all weapons which are presently "sucking our blood" will be gradually eradicated and humanity, along with its leaders, will come to understand that weapons are no longer needed to solve our problems.

It is also possible that between 1997-2025 Christ will reappear with certain Angels, and certain of His Disciples, and guide humanity toward a new dimension of consciousness.

Many agents of darkness and their servants try to convince humanity that the end of the world is near, that humanity will never learn cooperation, that peace will never come, that greater suffering, pain, and starvation are on the way.

The agents of darkness never give us a bright picture, and by spreading such pessimistic, negative thoughtforms, they pressure humanity to think and act along the lines of destruction, death, suffering, and pain.

Once the gears of the human mind are engaged in such negative, ugly, destructive thoughts, humanity will be forced to live in such a way that it will fall into danger in trying to actualize the prophecies of the agents of darkness.

At the present we need leaders who will bring us hope, optimism, and joy; tell us that the future will be bright; tell us that the human soul is alive and sound; tell us that humanity will pass the crises and will build a greater future. In spreading such a vision we will condition the thinking of humanity and lead it into positive lines — "Whatever man thinks in his heart, so is he."

Give vision to people and people will actualize the vision.

The second forecast for the year 2025 is that politicians all over the world will deeply sense their responsibility for humanity and Nature, and in special schools they will study the science of mission, the science of responsibility, and the science of willpower.

After 2025 we will have more enlightened leaders and politicians who will live for their mission with self-forgetfulness, a sense of reponsibility, and will be armed with the spirit of good for all.

The Great Ones gave us the Great Invocation in which is stated, "Let Purpose guide the little wills of men." Future politicians will try to understand this Purpose and try to guide people according to that Purpose, to that Will.

One of the sacred duties of a politician will be to study the Law of Reincarnation and the Law of Karma and think, feel, speak, and act under these two major laws of the Universe.

Reincarnation is the process through which worlds come into being, and, after a degree of unfoldment, they disappear to reappear once again according to the life they demonstrated in the past. In the light of the Law of Reincarnation, the politicians will understand the true history of the past, present, and future and proceed accordingly.

Along with this law, the politicians will study the Law of Karma which will shed the brightest light on the evolution of humanity's past, present, and future events. Then politicians will organize their service in harmony with the Law of Karma.

Karma is not in itself an active principle, but it becomes active in response to our actions. We receive from karma what we give to it. By our actions on all levels we build our future life — our future bodies, our future relationships, and our future achievements and failures. Such an understanding puts pressure upon our soul to live a more conscious life in harmony with the universal Purpose.

People often think about the Will of God and say, "Whatever happens is the Will of God because nothing happens without the Will of God." And they think also, "Because the Will of God is omnipotent, no matter what we do, He will lead us to redemption, or to the destination He has for us in His mind."

But these statements are mixed with truth and falsehood. First of all, life shows us that we have a free will which we can use for destruction or for creativity. Of course, life has a destination, but it is not forced upon us. We have freedom to accept it or refuse it. In case we refuse, we annihilate ourselves in chaos. If we accept, we live a life leading us to that unknown destination.

The Law of Reincarnation exists to give us a chance to come to our senses by studying life from the viewpoint of cause and effect — karma.

Future politicians will not act under the force of ignorance but in the light of a pure knowledge of these two laws.

We are told that the majority of the human race will reach higher and higher levels of consciousness and will use that consciousness to have a better life in the future by eliminating those actions which are seeds of pain and suffering.

The integration and synthesis of humanity will continue in the next centuries and, of course, the integration and unification process of the world is watched by both totalitarians and forces of Light.

Totalitarianism will try by all means to take control of a unified humanity to use it for their self-interest, without knowing the fact that as humanity unifes it naturally casts away any totalitarian manipulations. Light automatically disperses darkness.

Two thousand years ago Christ said, "Thy Will be done." What is that Will, and how will it be "done"? We will see in the near future that books will be written and movies created to demonstrate this science. When we say, "Let Purpose guide the little wills of men," what is meant by "Purpose" and by our "little wills"? How are the "little wills" going to be guided by Purpose which is the expression or expansion of the Will of God? These questions will be answered and a science formulated to "guide" us in that Will.

Because the field of politics is First Ray, a politician's duty is to bring in the Will of God, the will-to-good for all humanity. To do so, he must educate the public by talking about the Will of God. Future politicians will be scientifically trained to bring the Will of God into the heart of humanity, and show them how to obey and follow the Will of God.

Humanity is currently like a factory whose foreman is untrained and the workers have no clear directions to follow. What kind of factory can there be under such circumstances? It is imperative for us to use our "little wills" to make our leaders guide us in the Will of God.

In thinking and hearing about these forecasts, we also amplify these ideas. Through our brain and thinking process, we mentally broadcast to the Universe that this science is developing — the Science of "Thy Will Be Done" that Christ introduced two thousand years ago.

The third forecast for the coming Age is that in the years 2030 to 2040 education will be totally dedicated to expanding the consciousness of humanity so that it becomes sensitive to all forms of life as a whole. Communication will be developed between man and animals, between man and trees, oceans, rivers, mountains . . . and stars. Mankind will become sensitive to all life.

There are films currently on the market which impress us with the idea that the destruction of our planet is inevitable. In the future, such films will not be shown. It is important to deny the entrance of such ideas into our consciousness because we must foster the spirit of optimism. Through optimism, the creative forces of Nature can work to influence people. This does not mean that we should blind ourselves to dangers but see dangers in their proper perspective. They are like small waves on a vast and beautiful ocean.

The fourth forecast for the future is that between the years 2025 and 2050 communication lines will be established between us, those who have passed away, and the Higher Worlds. Through the use of newly-developed instruments, it will be possible to speak with anyone who has died. You will say, "Father, how is everything?" and he will reply, "Don't worry; I am so happy. I can go anywhere, see everything, and listen to you." People living on earth will be able to do this by placing a small object that once belonged to the deceased in a machine which will register the soul frequency of its former owner. The machine will then tune to that frequency and put us in touch with those who are living in the subtle worlds. And, if the person we are trying to reach has reincarnated, that instrument will give us their "change of address" in the physical world where they are now living as infants and children.

Soul frequencies will be charted and categorized. For example, if a person's soul is five thousand years ahead, he will be a Group B soul, among Group D and F souls, and so on. His frequency will be mechanically determined and charted.

People who have passed away recognize in a short period of time that they have died, but they cannot communicate with us. They come around us when we miss them, but we do not see them. They can contact us telepathically, but this is not necromancy. It is not a case of bringing spirits down to lower levels through unlawful practices but electronically communicating with subtle levels where they dwell.

Even now our computers, telephones, radios, and televisions are becoming incredibly sophisticated. By taking the current rate of growth into consideration, we can see how in forty years our most sophisticated equipment will be like donkeys compared to the space shuttle.

Higher Worlds are those spheres in which Great Ones consciously function; these realms are great treasure houses, and we will be able to contact them when the need arises. For example, if an instructor is giving a lecture on compassion, he would be able to "place a call" to Lord Buddha, Who would then put him on hold and connect him to two or three disciples whose service it is to inspire and instruct on that particular subject.

At less sophisticated levels we are able to do this now any time we call a friend or a teacher and ask questions. In the future, we will be able to call the Higher Worlds.

There are millions of scientists who are now working on the "other side." Do not forget that there are seven Ashrams on the "other side" which have everything. Their machines are mentally built and work with mental matter, but the counterparts to these machines have filtered down to earth in much cruder versions. Our scientists need to build a bridge between "here and there."

This is why we need improvement; this is what we are working on. Improvement means to make the standard of a machine here on earth higher and higher until it is equal to its prototype in the higher planes.

If we made it to the moon, why is this not possible? Fifty years ago if a person had said that a Russian cosmonaut would successfully circle the earth for one year, people would have said it was impossible. A great Master advises us to remove the word "impossibility" from our dictionaries as it is considered the most hideous word. There is no impossibility; there is always possibility. _God is possibility;_ the best name for God is Possibility!

Along with these scientifically created devices, we will also be able to visit our beloved ones in our subtle bodies. Even now some people are under training to master this power.

The fifth forecast concerns the field of art. Between the years 2045 and 2055, art will reveal the beauty of the Cosmos in Its motion, color, sound, and rays. It will be possible to see the color of a planet as it revolves and rotates, experience the sound, color, and motion that it creates in relation to our galaxy and other galaxies. Art will demonstrate these things.

There is a Sufi dance which dramatizes the sun, moon, and planets dancing together. By experiencing the movements, colors, and music of the dance, a person is elevated to higher dimensions, becoming so dreamy, wondering what it all is. Such a dance is just a small indication of the kinds of art that will develop in the future.

The galaxies have colors, dances, and events occurring of such power and magnitude that if they were seen by human eyes the God within us would burst out. Art will be the agent of such an experience, instead of creating distortions and monsters to hang on walls.

The sixth forecast is that by the year 2050 science will have constructed globes, small earths in the solar system on which people can live, just as we currently live on our planet. The prototype of this idea is already present in the consciousness of humanity. These small planets will eventually hold as many as a million people. The atmospheres will not be regulated by space suits but by some type of electrical emanations that will control the air pressure and content of the external atmosphere.

M.M. says that these kinds of mechanisms already exist in the Ashrams but that they will not be given to humanity until it develops goodwill.

The seventh forecast concerns the field of religion. Religion will be dedicated to the emancipation of the soul from its vehicles, allowing it to exercise the power of omnipresence. We are now like an oyster which is attached to its shell; we think our bodies and clothes are us. In the future, religion will teach us how to leave the physical body and use the astral, mental, or higher bodies, as was taught in Egyptian mysteries in the pyramids. Religion will no longer be centered around psalms and hymns.

Each body is a vehicle which travels in a corresponding sphere of greater light. When a person travels using the astral body, he flies ten times faster than light. But if he uses the intuitional body, he travels ten thousand times faster. M.M. tells us that the Hierarchy does not wait for machines to transport Them from Earth to Venus; They can travel the distance in one second. If the meeting is changed to Uranus, They can also arrive there in a second.

This science will eventually develop. Great spiritual Initiates will teach men how to leave their bodies and penetrate into higher, corresponding spheres. Each sphere will be a university for us to learn various subjects. On each sphere we will learn something higher so that the God within us unfolds further.

Such a vision brings us serenity and hope for the future. It removes the poison that is currently circulating in our consciousness by saying, "No matter how things seem now, there is hope and beauty in the future, in spite of what happens in life."

One of our greatest obstacles is that we become so involved in our petty pains and sufferings that we cannot see beyond our own nose. We used to think that we were the Cosmos and that nothing else existed. As soon as we think about the Cosmos, we become balanced. Now we are balancing our consciousness and finding an equilibrium in living.

Mankind will someday be able to exercise its powerful omnipresence. We read that God is omniscient, omnipotent, omnipresent — all-knowing, all-powerful, everywhere. If God is this, what about His sons? His sons will be like this also — and we are His sons.

Omnipresence is the immediate ability to "tune in" to someone who lives in another city or country, or to be there with your etheric or mental body. You will see, talk, and return. Each person will get into his mental body and say, "Hi, what's happening?" Perhaps there is an exhibition you would like to see in China. You just get into your subtle bodies or into your intuitional body and see the people, float over the exhibits, and return.

Blavatsky had a disciple named Damodar who had this ability. Once, while traveling on a train several thousand miles away, he had the feeling that something had happened to her. He said to his companion, "I am going to sleep for a few minutes," and he left and went to visit Blavatsky. He returned a few minutes later and remarked to his companion,

"Blavatsky fell and broke her knees." They sent a telegram to confirm it — but Damodar did not need a telegram.

The forecasts and issues presented here are given in a general sense, without great detail, but they have far-reaching implications. If a person is free from time, space, and body, he has a million more possibilities to grow in his consciousness, in his heart, in the amount of information that is available to him, and in his abilities. He becomes like a son of God. This is why one of the great disciples said, "The whole Universe is waiting for the births of the children of God." All Nature waits for those who are maturing now to such a degree that they are no longer just consumers — eaters, sleepers, and fertilizers — but are slowly becoming angelic. Perhaps in the year 3000 we will look back at the primitive level in which humanity now finds itself and reflect on how ugly it was to have to eat and go to the bathroom!

The eighth forecast for the future is that white magic will be developed to such a degree that animals and other life-forms will be prepared to be initiated into the fourth kingdom. Millions of devas that have not yet gone through human evolution will eventually be brought into human incarnation. Most devas are born through flowers; some of them are birds. All must come to the human kingdom to develop intellect. As Blavatsky said, "All advanced intelligences pass through the human kingdom."

The white magic to which we refer is not slight-of-hand or an illusory trick. It is the science of using the higher mind in such a powerful way that each thought controls tremendously powerful energies and rays which can be directed toward various life-forms to release the divinity in them.

The divinity in animals is blocked and encapsulated. The Spirit exists in a dog, an elephant, or a cat, but in animal form; the Spirit has become the animal. Both the animal and human forms are a kind of prison. We are prisons in which Spirit is imprisoned. Solar Angels are sometimes referred to as "Exiles." How can those Prisoners be released?

White magic is going to influence the brain, certain centers, and the hidden programming contained within them which is not yet activated. In the smallest animal there is the programming of the Most High which says that it is going to become a man, an angel, and then an Archangel. But this programming is deeply buried, and no one knows how to put it into action. White magic will be able to push certain "buttons," and then the animals will be able to recognize their purpose.

White magic used in this way will not interfere with the natural individualization process that animals and people go through. Life conditions itself. You can destroy or build yourself; it is in your hands. It will be the task of future white magicians to burn the trash that is accumulated in our "stables" and create purity. The three Magi Who saw the star and followed it to where Christ was to be born are a kind of White Magician. But future Magi will be ten thousand times more advanced. It is not a matter of interference because Their actions will all be under law. Whatever is asked is given. If a person asks for the devil, he will come; if he asks for an angel, one will come. It will all be programmed. The task is to find the right program.

White magic will also enable us to direct Light in such a way that retarded children will be able to find their balance and equilibrium, their sanity and clarity, and become advancing students. The virtues and other hidden potentials within a person will be brought out.

God's Will and Purpose are programmed and tucked into our pocket, our computer, and are going to be brought into manifestation. When a person is born, he is like an acorn; he is a little "something" which contains the entire oak tree. That "something" is the program which is within. If the right environment is provided, the acorn will become a huge oak tree. A human being is programmed to be a god. In Psalms it is written that we are gods. But when Christ recited this psalm to the people, they became very angry and asked, "How can a man become God?" Yet it is found in all holy scriptures that humans are potential gods.

The ninth forecast is that by the year 2075 all disease will disappear. An energy ray will be discovered that will heal every kind of disease. A person will enter a small chamber filled with the energy of this special ray and emerge totally purified. All viruses, microbes, and bacteria found within the physical, emotional, and mental bodies will be removed. It will be possible to see this "dirt" leaving the bodies. A great vacuum cleaner will gather it and convert it into fertilizer.

It will come about that if an Initiate decides he can no longer use the body he has, he will leave it and take a new one. For example, if he wants to be a little taller, with darker hair, and so on, he will take such a body to fit himself to future responsibilities.

Death will totally disappear. We will not need graveyards. Graves are proof that humanity is stupid. If it were not for our stupidity, we would not need graves. We have committed so many wrongs for millions of ages that we are digging our own graves. The idea of a graveyard defeats the Godliness within. Christ said, "O death, where is thy sting? O grave, where is thy power?" There is no power in death. Death will no longer have power over us because death cannot have power over God.

The tenth forecast is that in or about the year 2080 fear, hatred, anger, jealousy, revenge, and greed will no longer exist. These gophers are eating our roots. We punish ourselves with fear, hatred, anger, jealousy, revenge, and greed.

The absence of negative emotions and thoughts does not mean that the Lords of Karma will be out of a job. The Law of Cause and Effect will always operate, but, instead of operating for our transgressions, it will operate for our labor of Light. For example, if a person kills someone, this is karma. But if he teaches someone instead, this is also karma.

Karma will become white magic. It is cause and effect which is found in many forms on many levels. Instead of producing negative results, it can produce positive results. A person could save the lives of five hundred people, and then a thousand years later those people would become his teachers. He will have this opportunity because he saved them.

It is important to look to the future with optimism and not take things in a limited perspective. Remember the words from *The Legend of Shamballa*: "The dawn is minutes away." Waves keep hitting us, one after another, but we can begin each new year with beautiful visions. We will be able to close our eyes, die, and return in 2080 when people no longer hate one another. We will come back wondering, "What strange world is this? There is no fear? How did this happen?"

We sometimes think that without fear and anger we do not exist, that a relationship between a man and a woman without jealousy is nonsense, and that revenge is the power of man. What will exist in their stead? *Love!*

The eleventh forecast is that in the year 2085 the Solar Angel will be video-taped so that a person can see his Angel.

With this breakthrough, loneliness will disappear. Loneliness is one of the greatest traps on the Path. Loneliness is a great enemy which traps us every moment. Because we are trapped in loneliness, we do the most destructive things in the world. When loneliness is gone, a person will realize that he has everything within himself and that he is complete. By going very deeply into these ideas, we can find how true they are.

In *The Legend of Shamballa,* we find mentioned that loneliness is one of the gates to Shamballa. The kind of loneliness referred to in this instance means the power of a detached attitude in which nothing can impose its will upon a person or side-track him from the Path. This reference does not take loneliness in the usual sense but challenges us to understand what loneliness means esoterically.

Loneliness, as commonly understood, is a craving to have someone around to lean upon or to support. People often think that if they do not have others around for these purposes, they are lonely.

The twelfth forecast is that the human soul, or spirit, will be photographed in the heart center of each man. This will happen around the year 2145 A.D. It will be possible to see your real face, in addition to the bodies, glamors, illusions, as well as the Soul. This was referred to in the New Testament: "We see Him as if in a mirror, but later we will see Him face to face."

Starting with the year 2200, the majority of the people under the guidance of Great Ones will learn to leave their physical bodies consciously.

In 2250 they will learn to leave their astral bodies.

In 2300 they will leave their mental bodies.

During these three hundred years, they will learn how to build the Temple, or the Lotus, within their higher mind and use the energies of light, love, and sacrifice.

In 2400 a great amount of people will become Arhats and their consciousness will be focused in the Intuitional Plane.

Starting in 2500 some major groups will live as Triads. They will actualize their True Self in light, in love, and in beauty or sacrifice.

From 2600 to 2700 they will start building their intuitional and atmic bodies and communicate with the corresponding planes of the solar system.

From 2700 to 3000 the Hierarchical Plan will be totally fulfilled, and the Spiritual King will achieve His Purpose.

The dates given here are not fixed dates by prophets. The destiny of humanity is in its own hands. Dates may change from 10 to 100 years according to the responses or reactions of humanity to the inpouring of energies.

The Teacher said: "It is the human thoughts, striving, and visions that will create the 'new.' "

"The "new" in this book is a "new" which, since the beginning of this century, has been unfolding and blooming, as a seed unfolds and blooms into its flower.

Welcome to the Olympus of 3000 A.D.

Prelude

The Legend says
this world
has a Captain
and He is called
the Lord of the World,
the Eternal Youth,
Sanat Kumara.

He has a great Council
with very, very advanced,
superhuman Beings.

Then there is the Hierarchy,
the Church Invisible,
the group of the Masters
of Wisdom,
the enlightened
Sons of man.

This Hierarchy
has three major departments
which are called the departments of
willpower,
love-wisdom,
active intelligence.

The heads of these departments
are three Jewels
in the Hierarchy.

The Hierarchy
is divided into
seven groups.
These groups
are called
great Ashrams.

The first Ashram
deals with politics;
the second, with education;
the third, with philosophy
or communication.
The fourth one is
the source of inspiration

for the arts
and also creates
harmony through conflict.
The fifth one is for
concrete science.
The sixth one
is religion.
The seventh one
deals with economy,
finance, rules, orders,
and ceremonies.

This Legend
is written
for the future
of humanity.

The future of humanity
is the result
of the Purpose
of the Lord,
the result
of the Plan
of the Hierarchy,
the result
of the heavy labor

of humanity,
the result
of all our aspirations
and strivings,
the result
of all our selfless service
for each other,
and of
our sacrifices to attain the Future.

The Great Council

The Inner Council Chamber of Shamballa
was sitting
as a seven pointed
ruby star of fire.

There were three
ancient Beings with Lotus eyes,
and in front of Them. . .
the King.

In front of the King
there were the three Lights
Who were like
shining wheels of seven colors.
The scriptures call Them
by various names.
They are the three Buddhas
Who are the gears

of all wheels of motion
in the world.

Around these stars
there were circles
of Beings
like huge multicolor
diamonds.

This was the Council
Chamber
of Shamballa,
the household
of the Father.

It was a full moon
in May, 3000 A.D.
The great Lord
of the World
called
the three great Flames
of the three departments
of the Hierarchy
and the seven Leaders
of the Seven Rays

to His Council Chamber —
Shamballa —
and said:

> *My Warriors,*
> *My Spirit*
> *is content*
> *with what You did*
> *for this tiny planet*
> *in the vast Space.*
>
> *The rays of the Sun*
> *are now dancing in a circle*
> *in each atom,*
> *in each form,*
> *in each man.*
>
> *The square is broken,*
> *the triangle is surpassed,*
> *and the circle reigns*
> *in its majestic symphony.*
>
> *The Earth*
> *is now sailing*
> *within*
> *billions of*

electrical rings
of the rays
of the Sun.

The timetable
of evolution
was met
quite closely,
and the pulse of the
Central Spiritual Sun
is felt
within the heart
of each form.

Thus, the Cosmic Magnet
will initiate
a new rhythm
in the life
of the planet,
raising the planet
another rung,
in due time,
on the ladder
of another
fiery round . . . .

My Warriors,
throughout all the centuries
My Heart
was within Your hearts,
keeping Your steps
on the path
of service
synchronous with
the rhythm
of the Heart of the Cosmos.

And now
a new star
is shining
upon the head
of each of
My Warriors.

Because of Your
undivided
fiery labor,
You are able
to expand
a little more
into the
Cosmic Presence.

Very soon
You will be called
to a greater,
more daring
labor
on the path
of Infinity
to demonstrate
the greater Beauty
of Your innate Divinity.
Thus, a deeper layer
of Your Inner Glory
will be revealed
unto You.

And as You go
from glory to glory,
You will spread
in Your fields of labor
greater harmony,
greater beauty,
greater power,
and greater,
greater simplicity.

Many, many sons of men
are ready

_to take the plough
into their hands
which You
so wisely used
to cultivate
the fields
of all human endeavors._

_The Great Council
wants to hear
Your reports
and then set
new directions
for an even greater
Future._

_First I want
the reports
of My three Diamonds
in the Hierarchy Who,
as a Triangle of Fire,
transmitted
My inspiration
to the seven Ashrams
on the Seven Rays._

And now
My beloved Son,
Who was able
to penetrate
through all the layers
of maya
and resurrect
the Divinity
within Himself
for the first time
in the history
of the planet,
and Who has performed
sacrificial service
for the One Life
throughout all His days;
He Whose blood
throughout ages
drop by drop
changed into
roses
and bloomed
in the aura
of all faithful co-workers;
Whose labor created
many, many cultures
and civilizations

and built
the bridge
for the first time
between the Father
and the Son,
between the Heart of the Cosmos
and the heart of man —
He is to give
His report
to this Council
of Shamballa.

The Commander

There was silence
in the Chamber
of the Lord.

All the eyes
of the great Warriors
turned toward
the Commander
of the Army
of Light —
the Aquarius,
the Christ.

He was a pillar
of white flame
around Whom
a rainbow

was flowing
in spirals.

　　　　"Father,
　　　　It was Your Will
　　　　I tried to awaken
　　　　in all men.
　　　　I tried to release
　　　　Your Presence
　　　　through Me,
　　　　unobscured.

　　　　"It was Your Will
　　　　which became
　　　　the ladder of ascent
　　　　for Me
　　　　and for
　　　　My brothers.

　　　　"Through Your Will,
　　　　every step
　　　　brought us closer
　　　　to our essential
　　　　Self
　　　　in which Your Eyes

shone more and more,
inspiring courage,
service, and sacrifice,
revealing
deeper layers
of Your Purpose.

"All Sparks of Life
gradually responded
to Your call,
and chaos became Beauty.

"We are again
on the Path
of our
Cosmic destiny.

"In all My labor,
My Brothers
in the Fiery Triangle
and in all Ashrams
worked and served
as a symphony
in greater

and greater
cooperation.

"In Our cooperation
We learned
the secrets of
the Law of Synthesis,
which was
the compass needle
of Your Purpose.

"We learned to live
in Your Purpose,
to serve
in Your Purpose,
and to know
Your Purpose
as the highest,
the supreme Good
for every Spark,
in every Spark
in the living,
loving
Fire.

"In all Your Ashrams
the Hierarchy,
for all these
millions of years,
has never stopped
using the sword
of Your fiery
Will.

   "It is
   by this sword
   that We initiated
   Your disciples
   into the field
   of service,
   dedication,
   and total renunciation.

   "By this sword
   We built the Path
   for pilgrims
   toward Home.

   "By this sword
   We protected

humanity
from the arrows
of intense power
thrown into
Our spheres
by the dark lodge
and directed
by its agents
to this planet.

"In all Our endeavors
We worked for
one thing —
to reveal Your Will
and condition humanity
to cooperate
and then
be one
with that Will.

"We eventually
established
the sacred ceremonies
of Initiations,
and,
My Lord,

for the first time
in the history of humanity
people saw
the Rod of your Servant
and Your Rod
with flaming diamonds
made by the fire
of lightning.
They saw these Rods
operating to unfold
certain petals of the Lotus,
even to destroy
the petals
and release the Jewel.

"What an honor it is,
My Lord,
for humanity
to witness these ceremonies,
see the Rods
in the ceremonies of Initiation,
and aspire to be one
of the Initiates.

"We used the Fire of Love
and the Light of Cosmic

mental electricity
to enlighten
the whole planet
and to make
every unit of Life
realize that
humanity as a whole
is one entity
traveling
to higher spheres
of the Solar System,
of the Galaxy —
to the Universe
and beyond. . . .

"Throughout ages
the blood of
Your Warriors
was shed
upon the road of Life,
upon the deserts of ignorance,
and upon the rocks
of human pride,
greed, and selfishness.

"But from each
drop of blood
a new life
streamed forth,
a new hero
was born,
a new fire
was kindled,
and new labor,
new striving,
new, new arrows
of aspiration,
dedication,
and decision
pierced
the blanket of darkness
around the Earth.

"Humanity —
Our garden —
at last began to bloom,
and it was
a great joy and bliss
to see Our labor
growing like a
full-blooming garden

from the mud
to lofty levels
of existence.

"Very soon
We noticed
that every Ashram
on subjective levels
and even the Tower,
O Lord,
was surrounded
with blooming flowers
of every beauty.

"We knew
humanity
would triumph
because Your Heart
was pulsating
in each heart.

"Our great,
great gratitude
to You,
Father,

for Your great sacrifice
which allowed
all Sparks
living on this planet
to find the way
Home.

"Our gratitude
to Your silent co-workers
who throughout the ages
helped the planet,
the great Kumaras,
the great Messengers
from the Solar System
and the Galaxy,
and to the Lord Buddha
Who synchronized
Our heartbeat
with the pulse
of Your Purpose
for centuries
and provided
energy for Us.
Our gratitude to Them.

"Accept Our labor,
O Lord.

"All Sparks of Life
are joining us today
to express gratitude
for Your agelong
sacrifice.

"Glory, glory,
glory
to Thee,
Father."

There reigned
a deep silence
in the Tower.

In that silence,
the symphony of synthesis
burst forth
like Cosmic fireworks
of color and form.

Then Christ continued:

> "My Co-workers of
> the Fiery Triangle
> in the Hierarchy —
> the Lord Manu and
> the Lord of Civilization —
> will report
> each in His turn."

The Lord of the World,
Melchizedek,
Who was sitting
in a golden, radiating Lotus
with petals of fire,
responded:

> *Your labor is recorded*
> *by the great*
> *Lords of Karma.*
> *Your labor*
> *is the power*
> *lifting You toward*
> *future achievements*
> *in Our Solar System.*

There will be a place
for You
to be a part
of the Chalice
of the great, great
Almighty Lord
of Seven Solar Systems
where You will demonstrate
greater sacrifice.

Now, My Warrior,
Manu,
let Us hear
from You.

The Manu

"My Lord,
it was a difficult labor
to carry Your Will
throughout
races,
nations,
kingdoms of Nature,
and great planetary groupings.

"But We did it.
We inspired
people on Earth
to come together
and solve
their differences
and create groups —
larger and more integrated.

"We inspired
the leaders of these groups
to integrate and synthesize
the little groups
into a greater whole
until We had
the United Nations.
This was the seed
of the present world government
which is in contact
with the Ashram
of the First Ray.

"Now We have
one world.
There are no boundaries;
there are no passports.
Anyone can go
anywhere in the world
and feel at home.

"There is a great
mixture of the races.
They all feel as one.
And because of this union,

the health of humanity
is fundamentally improved.

"We were forced
to wipe out some
areas of pollution.

"We moved many areas
into the ocean
and elevated
purified lands
from the bottom
of the sea.

"Those who were
karmically ripe
perished by the millions.

"Parts of the
submerged continents
were on the west coast
of Canada
as well as parts of the land
called the United States.

"Parts were in
the Middle East and
in the Mediterranean.

"Part was in Japan
and its environs.

"Some in Central Asia
and South America.

"We now have
new lands
in many oceans,
especially the ocean
called the Pacific.
These lands are good
for habitation
and for higher culture.

"The chemical pollution
of the Earth and humans
disturbed the balance
of energies
controlling the planet.

"We brought new energies
from a few constellations
and released them
upon the Earth.

"This created
a new response
in the brain
of humanity.
Humans responded
in better ways
to the Law of
Group Progress."

It is fitting
that the Lord of Civilization
should continue.

The Lord of Civilization

The Lord of Civilization,
Who works under
the major Third Ray,
and operates Rays Four, Five,
Six, and Seven —
stood up
and with great reverence said:

"My Lord,
We worked
primarily through culture.
We tried through
all Our Ashrams
to enlighten
the minds of men
and to release
the light buried
under heavy layers
of prejudice,

superstition,
illusion,
ignorance, and greed.

"The release
of this light
created
the new civilization
We have today.

"It would be proper
if, My Lord,
each Leader
of the major Ashrams
spoke for Himself."

The Lord of the World
kept silent
for a while.
Then, turning to
the future Manu,
the Rajput Prince,
He said:

My King Warrior,
this august Council
will hear You.

The First Ray Ashram

The great Prince,
a pillar of ruby light,
said:

> "My Lord,
> at last We were able
> to formulate the Law
> for all nations
> and make leaders observe
> the One Law
> for the planet.

> "My Lord,
> We were able,
> after very hard work,
> to emancipate women
> from the slavery of men
> and from the slavery

of their own glamors
to act like men.
Now the feminine principle
is in full bloom
and the masculine principle
is in full glory.

"One of Our tasks
was to inform
the leaders of all nations
about the accumulating
dangers. . . .

"My Lord,
some leaders
were so blinded
by their power,
luxury, and ignorance
that We could not
help them immediately.

"Often after Our warnings
a tidal wave of danger
would come and
wipe them out.

"We often lost
great co-workers,
messengers on this path
of service. . .
but We did not give up
Our efforts
to impress the need
of a new civilization
and a new culture
on the brain
of mankind.

"My Lord,
We were on guard
every minute
during all these centuries
in order to destroy
all that impeded
the synthesis of the races.

"The children of Earth
needed heavy labor
to see
the path of unity.

"We worked mostly
with statesmen
all over the world.
Decade after decade
We sowed the seeds
of unity
and synthesis
in their minds.

"The Lord Agni
and many hundreds of devas
on the mental plane
helped Us.

"We had great difficulties
with those who were stuck
in their racial superiority
or so-called nationalism.
But, eventually,
they started to see
beyond themselves,
and the integration
of the races of man
began.

"My Lord
one of Our labors was
to destroy the cloud
enveloping the Earth,
a cloud which was
acting like a satellite
transmitting to humanity
all forms of evil.

"This cloud, My Lord,
was formed in Space
from all the evil intentions
of members of humanity
expressed through their thoughts,
words, and actions,
and like a great vampire
it was sucking the joy
of humanity.

"Now people are free
from the transmissions
of this satellite cloud
and can think
clearly,
in harmony

with the highest good
for humanity.

"We moved great masses
of people
from place to place
to help the fusion
of the races.

"Now We have
one race,
one humanity,
with one main global language,
and each member
of humanity
is proud
to be a part
of one humanity.

"Thus We eliminated
the great waste
of armaments
which was sucking
the lifeblood
of humanity

and which was a great
contributing factor
to pollution,
disease,
and suffering.

    "Ending wars
    between nations
    improved the health
    of the three vehicles
    of humanity
    and the health
    of the planet.

    "And all the resources
    went back to humanity
    to build
    their new civilization.

"We wiped away
all guns of every kind —
even from museums —
because the children
of the Future
were so disturbed

when historians explained
what man had done
with these guns
to his fellow
human beings.
The last museum of arms
was destroyed
by the citizens,
and museums of guns
are no longer
a part of their
history and culture.

"All submarines and warships
are now moving universities
upon the oceans of the Earth
in which great Initiates
teach
the wisdom of the Sun.

"The Teaching
We gave humanity
was the wisdom of Shamballa
filtered through
the Ashrams of the Masters.

"We gave the Teaching in three
phases —
the intellectual approach,
the intuitional approach, and
the will approach —
to integrate
the personality
and fuse it with
the Soul,
and then pass it beyond
to the awareness
of the Spark.

"We had many problems
with the so-called esoteric schools
in the world.
The most difficult task
for them
was to relinquish
things related
to the past level
of their evolution
and to press forward
with the new phase of the Teaching
and appropriate it

to the present level
of their evolution.

"The Teaching as a whole
was always under attack.
Agents of darkness
continuously tried
to mix it with illusion
through unclean channels,
prophets, and mediums.
They tried to create
chaos
in the minds of the weak,
fanaticism
in those who were glamored,
reaction
in those who sensed
but did not see the motive
behind the Teaching.

"We had difficulty
making people understand
the infallibility of
the Teaching of Light
in all ages
and not attack

the Teaching that was
necessarily conditioned
by the level
of one special Teacher
or by the level
of those to whom
the Teaching
was presented.

"We tried to keep
their attention on the substance
of the Teaching —
which always was,
is, and will be —
and to discard
the elements that were
superficial and limited
in time and space
to their level of attainment.

"This eventually developed
a discrimination
which became
the torch
in their hands

leading toward
Infinity.

"Agni Yoga,
the yoga of synthesis,
the yoga of life,
is now taught
in all schools.

"We have millions
of Agni Yogis,
those who live in the
fire of Purpose
and radiate
their essence
through their sacrificial
life,
and thus prepare themselves
for superhuman evolution.
Their consciousness
is now focused
in their Spiritual Triad.

"At the present
the wisdom of Shamballa —

the Fire —
is presented
to humanity
through the Light
of seven streams of power —
the Seven Rays.

"These Seven Rays,
which are the sources
of a sevenfold wisdom,
are presented
in all forms of education,
and humanity
is in closer contact
with the Source of these Rays.

"Thank You, My Lord,
for giving Me
this opportunity
to labor
for humanity."

Well done,
My Warrior of Old.
I need now to listen
to the Leader
of the second major Ashram,
Who had a great labor
and a mighty task
to prepare
for the coming
great cycle.

The Second Ray Ashram

The Lord of the Second Ray Ashram,
flooded with
pure blue light,
arose
and with great solemnity
said:

> "My Lord,
> We worked through
> what was called
> education.
> Through gradual revelation
> We made
> the hearts of men
> feel
> the unity of life.

"We tried to bridge
the hearts of men
to the Center
of the Heart of the Sun
and precipitate
compassion
into their hearts.

"We inspired
great philanthropic organizations
and thus paved the way
for world unity
and brotherhood.

"At present,
all schools
are organized
in such a way
that there is
one goal
higher than
specialization.
That goal is
to reach the stage
of continuity of consciousness
and discover the One Self.

"The thread of this Teaching
starts in kindergarten
and reaches to
Our Ashrams.

"All those who work
in education
are gradually impressed
more and more
by the Wisdom
of the Ages
provided to them
by the Hierarchy,
by the Ashrams,
and by specialized groups
in the Higher Worlds.

"Thus they are now
sensitive to
the call of Service,
the call of the advancing Plan,
and to the call
of the One Purpose.

"Thus humanity
is in the process
of fusion
with the Hierarchy.

"The servants of darkness
from Cosmic levels
tried hard
to keep these souls
in captivity
on the physical
and astral planes.
It was very difficult
for Us
to contact their souls
and relay to them
the Plan
of the Hierarchy.

"But eventually,
through hard work,
disciples from many fields
awakened the youth.

"One of Our great labors
was to release
many aspirants
from the traps of
narcotics,
tobacco,
and alcohol
in which they were caught
because of their
aspiration,
frustration,
and the heavy influence
of society.

"Today,
almost no one
uses alcohol.
Former manufacturers
of tobacco, alcohol,
and narcotics
are working hard
in different fields
to eliminate the karma
which they brought
to their path.

"With the elimination
of these three great enemies
to progress,
greater light penetrated
into the minds of men.

"They became goal-oriented;
they began to strive,
to labor,
to serve,
to sacrifice,
to live
not only for themselves
but also for others.

"We inspired
in all fields
of all Ashrams
the flame of education.
We confronted
great dangers
when, through education,
people tried
to use their knowledge
against each other.

"There was grave danger
when We released
the knowledge
from the Temples of Mysteries
to the masses through education.

"Today,
education is
the expansion of love and
the expansion of consciousness
to embrace
higher levels of being.
It is education
for sacrifice and service.

"Today,
education is in contact
with the Mind
of the Universe.
Education
is the steady process
of becoming
Oneself. . . .

"If You please,
My Lord,
may the Leader
of the Third Ray Ashram
continue?"

He may continue.

The Third Ray Ashram

And the Lord of the Third Ray,
dressed in a pure yellow
robe
with a five pointed
star
on His chest,
said:

> "My Lord,
> Our task
> was to make people
> think in the abstract mind
> through various philosophies
> which We provided
> through Our Initiates
> and disciples
> in the world.

"There was a great wall
between the lower
and the higher mind
of humanity.
We primarily tried
to bridge
that gap.

"We provided
the higher techniques of
intuitive thinking,
straight knowledge,
and pure reason,
analysis, and
synthesis.
Today
all humanity is able
to build the bridge
across this gap
between the worlds.

"Now,
any idea
can be rendered
practical,
and any experience

can be raised
into the ideal realms.

"We used, among others,
the Science of Impression
to bring ideas
from Higher Sources
to help humanity
feel,
recognize,
meditate,
and use
the ideas.

"Thus, year after year
the percentage
of those who were sensitive
to higher impressions
increased.

"And now
this greater
Science of Impression
is taught
in schools

through various ways —
through color,
through motion,
through dance.

"A great number of men
are so sensitive
that they do not need
the communication mechanisms
of past ages.
For them,
telepathy has replaced
the telephone;
clairvoyance has replaced
television.

"Very often
children now wonder about
the ignorance of
their forefathers
who allowed
a history of war
to exist,
causing destruction,
unjust discrimination,
and crime.

"It is now
really difficult
to make the children understand
that in olden times
a man got a knife
and killed another man,
or that warplanes
or rockets
bombed cities
and destroyed
life and objects.

"Sometimes when they see
any means of security
such as locks,
they laugh
and laugh.

"My Lord,
the world will never
return to the conditions
which We witnessed
for so many
thousands of years.

"There were
hardened elements
in the race of men
who always stood
against Our plans.

"They were
in all nations,
in all races,
in all countries.

"They were those
who were stuck
in matter,
in the body, in sex,
in property,
in money.

"But now the same souls,
once released
from their old glamors
and illusions,
are the servants
of humanity. . . .

"I wish, My Lord,
to let the Leader
of the Fourth Ray Ashram
continue."

Let Him continue.

The Fourth Ray Ashram

And the Lord
of the Fourth Ray,
dressed in a green robe
with a rainbow
on His chest
said:

"My Lord,
We tried
to synthesize nations
through Beauty:
beauty in form,
beauty in sound,
beauty in color,
beauty in movement,
beauty of Nature,
beauty of ethics,
beauty of the Plan,

beauty of service,
beauty of sacrifice.

"We used all these beauties
throughout ages.
Through Our Initiates
and disciples,
eventually
We were able
to awaken
the Beauty sleeping
in each man,
the Beauty of
the Divine Presence
in each man.

"Our theaters
are in the forests,
on mountaintops,
on the shores
of the oceans.
Through art,
We teach
the mystery of creation,
the mystery of the Cosmos,
the mystery of the

energy interchange
of planets,
solar systems,
galaxies.
Our art is now
the mirror
of the Future.

"In art,
people see the possibility
of their future achievement.
They see their divinity
on the path
of perfection.

"In the great dramas
of life,
the human beings
now can see
how the Cosmic creative forces
are in action.

"All that We do
on the Fourth Ray
has the goal

of releasing,
stage by stage,
the Inner Glory
in all people
so that they hear
the symphony
of the stars
in their hearts.

"Art has become
their daily bread;
schools, houses, and buildings
of the world
are works
of real art
built under a plan
that creates
a Cosmic symphony
or drama
when looked at
collectively.

"We taught humanity
the secret of music
through which they now
can heal any condition,

whether it is physical
or social.
Through music
they can tune to
any level
of consciousness,
any planet,
or any center
on the planet
and use this contact
to achieve a greater
perfection
in their beingness.

"There is a great, great
ongoing labor
on the planet.
Everyone has
caught the vision
of the Future.

"In olden times,
people were bound
to the past.
They used to gossip,
criticize, slander,

and belittle each other,
or sink into
the memories of
the past.

"Then they became
the slaves of
the so-called present.
All they did
was to save
their own skins —
and work
and dream
that they existed.

"At the present,
everyone thinks through
the Future.
They eventually learned
that the cause
of all improvement,
the cause
of all true labor and striving,
was the Future —
is the Future.

"And We tried
to put the vision
of the Future
in their hearts.
Every work of art
at present
is a book
of instruction.

"Now,
artists cannot understand
why in the past age
people created
art for the sake
of art.
Now art is
a magical means
of revelation,
of transformation
and transfiguration.
We even use art
for minerals,
for plants
and animals.

"The initiation of
the Sparks
in all living forms
was carried
on the wings of fiery art. . . .

"But, My Lord,
let the Leader
of the Fifth Ray Ashram
continue about
all of this."

*My Warrior
of the Fifth Ray,
You may continue.*

The Fifth Ray Ashram

The Fifth Ray Lord,
Whom They called
the Rose of God,
wearing a robe
of orange,
indigo, and yellow colors
and with a symbol of a flame
upon His chest,
approached the Great Lord
and said:

"My Lord,
We worked very closely
with all Ashrams.
We tried to penetrate
into the light
of the Fifth Ray
and cyclically reveal
the depth of knowledge

of the energies, forces,
laws, and principles
of the Cosmos
and relate them
to the need
of Our planetary
humanity.

"We proceeded
a long way.
Most of Our Initiates
and disciples
carried on this labor
while enduring persecution
and while under fire.
But We did it;
We created the all inclusive
and pure science.

"We created
great, great institutions
of research,
of facts,
of laws
and energies.

"Further, there was
a more difficult task
than that of discovery
and tapping into
the source of knowledge.

"Many, many human beings
delayed their progress
by misusing Our information,
or using it for
their own
destruction.

"We needed the help
of all Ashrams
to annihilate the danger
inherent in
misusing the knowledge
of discoveries.

"Every time
We gave them
a formula,
it was used
for the satisfaction

of their hatred,
their fear or pleasure,
or for their own
destruction.

"We were even informed
that the First Ray Ashram
had used many
ways
to destroy
the misusers.
In this way
We were relieved
of great tension.

"Very often
humanity reached
the edge
of self-annihilation
through Our discoveries.
But, with the help
of statesmen and diplomats
inspired by
the Second Ray Ashram,
once more
humanity was saved.

"We even had moments
where We thought
We must leave
this planet
and retreat.

"But humanity,
in a mysterious way,
acted righteously
and listened to
the Call of Life
coming from
the Tower,
O Lord of Life.

"We also had
great difficulty
passing Our discoveries on
to the right scientists
whose hearts
were in their rightful places
and who knew
how to safeguard
the secrets
so as not to leak them
from their minds.

"Dark forces
gave us the major difficulty
by dropping some secrets
into the brains
of those scientists who were
mediumistically inclined
and negatively oriented
toward human values.

"We were very careful
to pass on formulas of knowledge
according to the level
of achievement
of humanity.

"But dark forces
were very eager
to plant formulas
stolen from the brains
of careless scientists
into the brains
of those who,
without discrimination
and total knowledge,
would put them
on the market

and cause great hindrances
on the path of progress
of humanity.

"Thus,
many scientific discoveries
were premature,
unripe,
outside the context
of the overall picture
of the Plan.

"For example,
some medicines
cured illnesses,
then created
harmful reactions.
But if that medicine
had been given
one hundred years later —
because of newly-conditioned
bodies and psyches —
it would have been
totally helpful.

"Thus,
many beautiful people
were damaged.
Those who were
going to be great leaders
of humanity
were retarded
by the foresight
of the dark forces
and their agents.

"We learned that
the level of consciousness
and the level of beingness
must be considered
before any formula
is passed into the hands
of humanity.

"On one level
that formula
can be constructive;
on another level,
totally destructive.

"We impressed
upon the human mind
that
the mechanical achievements of science
should be parallel
to the actualization
and manifestation
of the inner glory
in man.

"All that science has created
are as shadows of the reality
existing in the spirit
of man.
Man must manifest
himself
eventually as a center
of omniscience,
omnipresence,
omnipotence.

"Man cannot
uplift his spirit
by flying at four thousand feet
or in the far off space.
Nor can he become clairvoyant

or clairaudient
by watching television.
A doctor cannot reach
conscious immortality
by depending on his knowledge
of the healing arts.
The power of omnipresence
cannot be actualized
by being in contact with
the other side of the world.
Man is equal to his
inner powers and virtues.
He expresses them
as his radiation,
as his fragrance.
Human beings
have all kinds of capacities
to be
unfolding flames
or radiant new dawns.

"They learned, my Lord,
that
more knowledge
or greater control
over Nature

or the collection of natural objects
does not lead them into freedom and joy
and Self-actualization.

"We saw scientists who,
at the end,
cursed all that they knew,
all that they had,
and those
who blessed the life
for all that they were.

"They learned, eventually,
that
artificially induced
changes
upon the living forms of Nature
were transgressions
against Nature —
whose consciousness is
millions of times greater
than the consciousness
of the little chemists
or doctors.
Eventually, my Lord,
people learned to cooperate

with Nature
and not interfere with
its dynamism.

"The greatest labor
We attempted
was to create
instruments which
eventually convinced
humanity that
there was an
etheric body,
there was
an aura
and chakras,
the Lotus,
and the Inner Dweller —
and, furthermore,
many unwanted guests
around man.

"Eventually We provided
the means to communicate
with those who left
their bodies.

This was done
with great scientific accuracy.

"Thus We eliminated
the fear of death
and much pain and suffering,
and their future consequences
were cast away.

"People now
can photograph
the departing soul of man;
they can photograph
the fiery flowers
of energies
in the vehicles of man;
they can even see
the glory of the human
soul. . . .

"Through these machines
the average human
can determine
the stage of evolution,
the stage of virtue

or sublimation
of any person,
and fit each one
to his or her
proper task
in the Plan.

"Through these machines
a man is
an open book.
He passes in front
of the machine,
and the Architects
see all They need
to see.

"All this has been done
to use human resources
more constructively
under the Law of Economy.

"We created these machines
by copying the inner structure
of the Third Eye.
But for a few

far-advanced disciples,
the machines became obsolete
as they developed
their own Eye
organically
and awakened
with highly clairvoyant eyes,
with highly clairaudient ears.

"We now have those
who can teach and demonstrate
the greater mysteries
of all seven senses.

"One of the most
successful paths
on Our line
is healing.
Healers rarely try now
to heal the dense body
directly.
Most of their work
is on the etheric body.

"They tune the etheric body
of the people
with the fire of electricity —
with the fire of love,
of wisdom,
of will.
These are the energies
They now use
to heal human vehicles
on three levels.

"Surgery is now
an obsolete science,
since humans understand
that the physical body
is the shadow
of the etheric prototype.

"Most humans at present,
knowing they are to go
to new tasks,
withdraw willingly,
leave their bodies,
and enter
into higher,

subtler planes
consciously.

"Their physical bodies
are burned to release
all elements of attachment
and contaminations.

"In this age,
We revealed to humanity
the secrets of the threefold electricity
under Your command,
My Lord. . . .

"I can continue longer,
if You want, My Lord,
but let Me close by saying
one more thing —
The world is now
free from the fear
of death,
and it is
further integrated
as one Brotherhood
of humanity."

The Presiding One said:

> *Very well done.*
> *And now I want to hear*
> *about the labor*
> *of the Leader*
> *of the Sixth Ray Ashram.*

The Sixth Ray Ashram

And the Lord of the Sixth Ray Ashram,
dressed in a robe
of silvery rose and red
and with the symbol
of a blue arrow
on His chest,
approached the Great Lord
and said:

"My Lord,
Our work was related
to the religions
of the world.
Cyclically We sent
Great Ones,
embodiments of Light and Love,
from our Ashrams
to guide humanity
on the path

of contact
with the highest
in man
and the Universe.

"But after We withdrew
the Messengers
back Home,
degeneration
of religion
took place
and the Temples
turned into bazaars.

"And this happened
everywhere,
every time
in the history
of humanity.

"Almost always
the Teaching We gave
was distorted
by human glamors,
fanaticism,

illusion,
desire,
and egotism
to such a degree
that it
completely manifested
in the lives
of many preachers
and religious leaders
as a hindrance
to the pure Teaching.

"We taught detachment;
they manifested
the worst forms
of attachment.

"We taught love;
they manifested hatred,
and eventually
religious leaders
created armies
standing against
each other.

"It was only
Our disciples,
scattered in all armies,
who eventually
formulated
in their minds
the blueprints
of a new
world religion.

"Then came
the days of thunder
and lightning,
the days of greatest
Revelations
when the Lord Christ
with His disciples,
and armed with thousands
of Angels,
began to walk again
on this Earth —
And men everywhere
saw Him
with great terror, hope,
ecstacy,
and a tremor. . . .

"His disciples and Angels
dispersed all over the world,
into all nations,
and spoke to people
of the glory hidden
in the heart of man.
They spoke of the One
Brotherhood of Humanity,
of the one religion
which everyone could
understand
according to his own
actualization of love. . . .

"Now, My Lord,
there is light,
there is Plan,
there is destination
in each heart.

"Humanity had never seen
the ceremonies now going on
in all solemnity
to initiate disciples
into higher consciousness,
expanding their awareness

toward the mysteries
of the Universe.

"His presence, My Lord,
gave birth to a
Universal Religion —
a bridge between humanity
and the Most
High Lord.

"This religion
was accepted
on the authority
of personal experience
and was based upon
the Sciences of Invocation,
Evocation, and Contact.

"Through these sciences
they were able
to receive wisdom
from Above
and energy
from Sources High.

"And now We
have
the world religion,
the Teaching of
the Hierarchy of Light,
which explains
the secrets of
total purification,
the secrets of
preparation for
higher initiations.

"At present,
in all temples and churches,
the Great Ones
are preparing
the aspirants
for the first and second
initiations,
presided over
by the great Lord,
Christ.

"These ceremonies
of initiation
use all the major discoveries

of the Fourth Ray Ashram,
the scientific technology
of the Fifth Ray Ashram,
and the scientific formulas
of ritual and ceremony
of the Seventh Ray Ashram.

"We initiate aspirants
into greater
responsibility,
striving, service,
and sacrifice
when they are ready
to meet the requirements
consciously.

"Thus We prepared
candidates for
major initiations.

"The cathedrals
of the world,
which were empty before,
are now filled
with initiates.

"The religion of
the Future,
which the Lord Christ
inspired,
has become
a dialogue between
the Almighty Presence
and man.

"The great buildings
of the Masons
are now used
consciously
to prepare men
for major breakthroughs
into Higher Worlds.

"We restored
the mysteries of all ages,
revealing through them
the deeper layers
of meaning
and significance.

"No conflict exists
at present
between any religion
because the new religion
revealed the essence
and the oneness
of all religions.

"The leaders
of religions
undergo
heavy education
and discipline
so that no blind one
teaches the blind.

"There is one university
in the world
for the Ministry,
and only those
who are ready
to hold the charge
of this Ashram
are able to go through
to receive

their certificate
for service.

"In this university,
many Masters
are Teachers.

"Our whole work
is to bring
humanity
under the jurisdiction
of the Head
of the Hierarchy —
the Christ —
so that
through Him
the Cosmic Principle
of Love
pours out and increases
in all departments
of Nature
in compassion,
simplicity,
beauty. . . .

"If possible, My Lord,
let the Leader
of the Seventh Ray Ashram
continue."

Let Him proceed.

The Seventh Ray Ashram

The Lord of the Seventh Ray Ashram,
dressed in a robe
of violet
and with a symbol
of three interlaced circles
of white
on His chest,
spoke:

"My great Lord,
Our Ashram
handled
the economic situation
in the world
and improved
financial interaction.

"As a result
of Our work,
all human beings
learned to share
consciously
whatever they had,
whatever they were,
whatever they knew.

"There is
a great abundance
on Earth
because of the
conscious use
of matter and energy.

"Everyone
has everything
he needs.
No one
is identified
with anything.

"And if anyone
needs something,

it is provided
for him.

"All the money from human labor
goes to the bank,
and anyone can
draw the amount
he needs.

"There is
one currency.
It never falls;
it never rises.
All these games
were the nightmares and fun
of the past.

"No one
accumulates money
because he has
whatever he needs.

"Greed, lies,
and exploitations

have been annihilated.
We express
gratitude to the labor
of all Ashrams.

"Our factories,
Our machines,
Our airplanes
and spaceships
do not make
noise.
Nor do they
radiate destructive
currents and
frequencies.

"At last
in the history
of humanity,
noise has been annihilated
and replaced
either with silence
or with
harmonious sound
or music.

"The Fifth Ray Ashram
brought great assistance
to this point.

"Also,
We have
no over-population,
as no one wants to marry
if he or she
is not of the standard
to give birth
to healthy bodies.

"Illegal relationships
are almost
non-existent
because the sex energy
is sublimated
to the throat center
and people have sex
only as a duty
to provide
the body
for a waiting soul.

"Through such
sublimation,
a great percentage
of the misery
which resulted
from marriage,
childbirth,
and divorce
is annihilated.

"The joy of
creativity
in higher realms
replaced the excitement of sex
in which human beings
were enslaved.

"Great Masters
in great universities
teach the mystery
of sex and marriage,
and all who will marry
must graduate
from these universities.

"The fires of
all lower centers
are sublimated
to their corresponding
higher centers,
and sex does not
present any problems
in this New Era.

"We also have
new ways
to use the fire
of Space
and the fire
of the Sun.

"The transportation machines
and all factories
work through these
combined energies.

"No pollution
is thrown
into the air,

into the water,
into the earth.

        "With the help
        of all Ashrams
        and with the Army
        of the great Lord Christ,
        the New Group of World Servers,
        with great difficulty
        We at last cleaned
        all pollution
        from the spheres
        of this planet,
        from its oceans
        and earth —
        a pollution
        which was almost
        endangering
        the life stream
        of the planet.

"We also had
much trouble with
monopolies —
with great, great

materialistic organizations
of many nations.

"It would not
have been as easy
for them to give up
if the arm
of the Lord
of the First Ray
had not helped them
understand
the vanity
of their attachments.

"Every new idea
We introduced
met with resistance
from great interests,
but then
the ways and means
were found
to make these new ideas
serve their interests.

"The First Ray Ashram
worked very closely
with Us.
It removed
all obstacles,
thus facilitating
the growth
of the Spirit
of the New Era.

"We created
ceremonies and rituals
to bring the Spirit
into closer relationship
with matter,
to enable the Spirit
to manifest
the glory
of the Cosmos
through every
developing, unfolding
form.

"I know, My Lord,
this is just the start
for all of Us.

"Another area
where We focused
Our attention
was the Brotherhood
of great heroes.

"We gave them
rituals and ceremonies
through which
they penetrated into
deeper understanding
of the work
of the great Architect
of the Universe.

"They opened to many
the beauty,
the wisdom,
the glory
of the Innermost Temple —
the Temple not made
by hands.

"Today their Ashrams
are centers

of great illumination
and transfiguration.

"In all Our work,
We had the help
of many Ashrams,
O Lord."

Then descended
once more
a deep silence
upon the Council Chamber
of Shamballa.

Around the assembly
of the Great Ones
were present Great Taras,
great women Masters and Chohans,
Who throughout ages
helped the Great Ones
achieve Their plans.

The Ancient of Days,
looking at Them,
said —

> *The most beautiful*
> *lilies in the Universe —*
> *with Your*
> *sacrificial and*
> *persistent labor,*
> *You vested*
> *rays of light*
> *in human form —*
> *shielded them, tempered them*
> *until they were ready*
> *to reveal their wisdom*
> *to humanity — and even to Angels.*
> *Thus throughout ages*
> *You provided currents*
> *of light and love and beauty*
> *to stream forth into the hearts*
> *of every Race —*
> *Glory to Thee. . .*
> *and gratitude*
> *from every living heart*
> *in Cosmos.*

The Future

And the Lord of the World
continued:

> There are three
> most immediate objectives
> to which I want
> to draw Your attention,
> My Warriors.
>
> The first is
> the Teaching of Will.
>
> > We must plan
> > and formulate
> > the ways and means
> > to create
> > new instructions
> > on Will
> > as intelligent, loving life force,

as energy,
as a link
between man
and the Center
where the Will of God
is known.

In all Ashrams
the subject of Will
must be analyzed,
penetrated,
and precipitated
into the ranks
of the New Group
of World Servers,
among which
You now have
many advanced
Initiates.

Of course,
there is always danger;
but Lord Christ
paved the way
with the energy
of His Love
which brought to humanity

*right human relations
and goodwill.*

*Now is the time
to distribute
on a great scale
the energy of Will
in all
human endeavors.*

*This will reveal
another layer
of the essential Divinity
in man.*

*This will enable
man to see
more clearly
in his heart
the Purpose
which the Masters
know and serve.*

*The second objective
is to prepare
the Ashrams*

for the departure
of Lord Buddha and Lord Christ
into higher spheres
of the Most, Most High.

   The Lord Christ
   will be replaced
   by the Warrior
   of the Second Ray.
   He will be the Annointed One,
   the Christ,
   for the new humanity.

Any move within the Universe
mobilizes chain reactions
for which You,
My Warriors, will be ready
until We lead this humanity
to its Seventh Round.

   Thus the Avatar of Sacrificial
   Love
   will leave Us
   when His work
   is consummated on Earth.

Great solar and zodiacal
ceremonies and rituals
will be enacted
for His glory
and expansion
at His next
Initiation with the Lord Buddha.

This will affect
every Spark of life
on the planet.

All will
recognize Him
as the Warrior,
the Conqueror,
and the Messenger
of God
and of man —
My Son.

This will last
nine years,
and the echoes
of these subjective festivities
will spread
as waves of higher culture

on the shores
of human life
in all departments.

This will uplift
all humanity,
and many will step
higher on the path
of evolution
and Infinity.

After nine years
Our Brother,
the Head of
the Second Ray Ashram,
will move
to the position
of the Christ,
the World Teacher.

And the Leader
of the First Ray Ashram
will occupy the position
of the Manu. . . .

Thus We will have
a constant moving on
and major labors
in the greater fields
of the Cosmos.

Never forget
that the Spark
within You,
the Real You,
will advance
into Infinity.

And each level
will be
more interesting
and challenging.

All departments
of human endeavor
will be led by one
of Your Initiates,
and thus the energy
of the Tower
will be spread
like a web
of electricity

into all systems
of activity.

It is after
this great fusion
that the Angels
Who guard the paths
of the Cosmos
will move and open
the gates,
and a new Cosmic Light
will shine
on the foreheads
of humanity.

That is why
the major task of Christ
was to teach
and to demonstrate
the mystery of Will,
the energy of Will,
the application of Will.

Be ready
for the final call
when We receive
the Cosmic Order.

_The trumpet of Shamballa
will announce
the dawn._

_Your next task
is to shield
humanity
from Cosmic evil._

_Be vigilant
on a Cosmic scale
to break the dark arrows
before they reach
the sphere of Earth._

_The Teaching of Will
to a great extent
will enable humanity
to fight
Cosmic evil,
and "to seal the door
where evil dwells."_

_There will be
danger of attack,
but every attack_

*will be a new call
for greater fusion
with Shamballa.*

*The Eye of Shamballa
will never sleep.
It will watch
every sign
coming from
the Cosmic depths.*

*Through the energy
of Will,
You will build
everywhere
the wiring of
the Aquarian Age.*

*Through this wiring
the power and fire
of Aquarius
will be transmitted
to every atom,
to every form
in the world.*

Within this light,
man will study
the Book of Life,
the Book of the
Essential Self.

The World Teacher
will explain
to humanity
the three phases
of Will.

> *First He will teach*
> *Will*
> *as expressed on*
> *the Cosmic Physical Plane.*
> *This will be*
> *for the general humanity.*
>
> *Then He will teach*
> *Will*
> *from the standpoint of*
> *the Cosmic Astral Plane.*
> *This will be*
> *for the advanced*
> *sons of men.*

Then He will teach
Will
from the standpoint of
the Cosmic Mental Plane.
This will be
for great Initiates.

The Teaching will give
You and humanity
all that is needed
to shield the planet
from the attacks
of dark forces
originating from
the Cosmic Astral Plane.

That is why
throughout the ages
there was an order
to develop
the energy of willpower
in humanity
through a life
of difficulty,
striving,
discipline,
and labor

*as preparation
for this phase.*

*For many centuries
the basic line
in all life activities
was to develop
Will
to "seal the door
where evil dwells."*

*It is Will
that masters —
and makes a man
a Master.*

*My Warriors,
these three tasks
confront You.
I know how ready
You are,
how accurately prepared
You are;
but I want to
remind You
about
eternal vigilance.*

Only through
eternal vigilance
does one become
an Eye,
an Initiate
on the Cosmic Mental Plane.

At present,
We have the command
of the Solar Lord
to sow the seeds
for the next
Solar System.

In the previous Solar System,
intelligence developed
to its highest degree.

In this Solar System,
the love aspect
of the Solar Lord
began to manifest
with its beauty.

In the next Solar System,
the will aspect

of the Solar Lord
will manifest
in its full glory.

Thus,
in the next Solar System
the Monads of Will
will take into Their hands
a greater role
in the labor
of evolution.

All this, of course,
will occur
in the distant, distant
Future —
but there is almost
no distance, in reality,
between now and
the Future.
There is only
the eternal **Now**. . . .

At this time
We must try
to plant the seeds
for millions of years

ahead,
seeing in each seed
the unfolding
of the next
Solar System.

Only in working
for the Future
will the tasks
of the present
be fulfilled.

The great Life,
the fiery Aquarius,
is pouring forth
His Waters of Life
upon the gardens
of the Future.

As We strive
to plant seeds
for the next
Solar System,
life on this globe
will improve
more rapidly
and create

a superior culture,
a superior
civilization.

> *The new culture*
> *will be*
> *the expression of*
> *the refined Intelligence,*
> *the expression of*
> *purest Love,*
> *and intelligent,*
> *loving Will.*
>
> *It will be*
> *the expression of contact*
> *with the Self within,*
> *of contact with*
> *Shamballa, the Father's Home.*
>
> *The new culture*
> *will be the path*
> *of the Transfiguration*
> *of humanity*
> *and a link with*
> *the values of*
> *the future culture.*

It is in the culture
that the highest strivings
of humanity
must be
reflected.

And because of
the unity
of the world,
the cultural fruits
of humanity
will belong
to all men
everywhere.

In olden days,
man worked six days
to meet his needs.
Now he works
three days to meet
his physical needs;
the rest — four days —
are dedicated to cultivating
the divine powers sleeping in him.

Culture is the food
of the inner man.

The Teachers of humanity
must inspire humanity
more and more
with real,
cultural striving,
a striving toward
the Cosmic Source of Fire.

The Divine Glory,
revealed in man
in a partial degree,
must express Itself
in Its total beauty.

Culture is
the manifestation and worship
of the Divine fire
in humanity.

Culture is
cooperation with
the creative fires
of Nature.

The integration
of humanity

within itself
and with Shamballa
will take place
only through
culture,
only through
fiery striving,
which is culture
itself.

The next step
is the delivery
to humanity
of the Science
of Relationship
or the Science
of Energies
between the stars
and man.

Now humanity
has incorporated
into its religion
the science of stars
and the effect
of their energies

on the centers
and life in general.

This was a great success
for My Warriors.
But a greater Teaching
must be forthcoming
about the Science of Energies.

It is time
for humanity to know
the real musical keys
of the zodiacal signs,
their corresponding colors,
centers, organs,
chemical elements,
and symbolic movements.

The Leaders of
the Seventh Ray Ashram,
in cooperation with
the Fourth, Fifth, and
Sixth Ray Ashrams,
must present
to humanity
rituals and ceremonies
which will enable

man to come
into greater contact
with zodiacal power sources
and use the signs
in their esoteric,
or reversed,
sequence.

Our aim
is to liberate
humanity
from its
planetary and solar
prisons.

The Fifth Ray Ashram
provided humanity
with the needed
inspiration
to build
spaceships.
But, now,
more economical methods
are required
to teach humanity
a space travel
by which

advanced groups —
not individuals —
will visit
other planets
and Solar Systems
in the Galaxy.

Humanity will even
be able to approach
within a certain vicinity
of Shamballa
and witness
in group formation
Its discoveries.

The true Teachers
of occult lore
were successful
in exposing
the many glamorous
clouds of those
who were impressed
with this part
of the Plan
but who,
because of strong glamors,
developed many systems

*of astral travel
or astral projection.*

> *To use
> the astral body
> as a vehicle
> of transportation
> was itself proof
> that they were
> travelers on the sea
> of glamor.*

*Real space travel
can now be introduced
to the members
of the New Group
of World Servers
because many of them
destroyed their
astral bodies
and conquered their
mental bodies.
Now they can stand
in the fiery sphere
of their
intuitional realms*

and begin
true space travel.

Only the fire
of Intuition
will protect the Self
from the destructive
forces in Space.

Earth travel
can be handled
on the higher mental plane;
but space travel
and travel in the Galaxy
need buddhic and atmic
vehicles.

We have another field
to work on.
In this last millenium,
human beings developed
consciously their etheric vision
as a result of their discipline
of purity.

Many of them
have astral and mental
clairvoyance.
It is now the time
to restore
the Third Eye
within all members
of humanity, the Eye
which, a long time ago,
was submerged
in the brain
as the pineal gland.

The etheric counterpart
of this Eye
still exists
in higher planes.
Some Initiates
are now ready
to be born
with Their Third Eye.

They will be born
in those hospitals
where the doctors
are also

occultists or
White Magicians.

In past centuries,
some of Them arrived
with Their Third Eye extant,
but the medical profession
considered such cases
abnormal and dangerous.

It will not be
considered so
in this and
coming centuries.
Those Who have
Their Third Eye
will be Leaders
in every section
of humanity.

In every school
We will have
an Initiate
with a Third Eye
Who will see
the mental life
of the students,

*also their karmic liabilities
and possibilities;
Who will record
the energy currents
affecting them
and detect the sources
of these currents
to stop or re-channel them,
if need be,
into other fields.*

*Very soon,
after thorough planning,
the curriculum
of this procedure
must be distributed
to the Leaders
of the New Group
of World Servers.*

*They will not only teach
about the Third Eye
but also
about the Eye — the Jewel
in the Lotus.
You must instruct
the Teachers of humanity*

how to contact the Jewel
in the Lotus
and release its glory.
As You know well,
the Jewel in the Lotus
is the Eye within the form
of man
of the Eye of the Solar Lord!

Let Us remember
that each Self
is an Eye
of the Solar Lord.

Expansion of
the vision of humanity
is the further unfoldment
of the great, great Eye
of the Solar Lord.

With all these duties
and responsibilities,
We have yet another
very serious
undertaking.

As We all know,
the door of initiation
will be open
to the animal kingdom
by the command
of the Solar Lord.

 Four species of animals,
 because of their
 age-long service,
 will be initiated
 slowly into
 the human kingdom.

  At first they will not
  create problems,
  but, as they increase in number,
  they will manifest
  their animal instincts
  and vices
  in varying colors
  and degrees.

  They will manifest
  violent emotions,
  urges, and drives
  left behind

by humanity
ages ago.

This will be
like bringing
a wild beast
into Your temple
at the time
of Your most sacred
ceremony.

How will You
deal with
these problems?
Because all of You
throughout the centuries
have collected
precious experience,
it is up to You
to organize
a proper Plan
to meet this problem
and keep this danger
to a minimal expression.

Do remember
that the presence

in the world
of so many
advanced Initiates
and the Hierarchy
will evoke
violent forces
from these
human animals.

These animals
were chosen
because of their service
and sacrifice
for human evolution:
the elephant,
the horse,
the dog,
the cat.

They must be
distributed intelligently
and with the full
cooperation of those
who will give birth
to them.

Many of them
will not make it
and will die
in the womb.
Many of them
will be attached
to their subtle forms.
Many of them
will not prefer
to come through humans.

For all these reasons,
great Ashrams
must establish classes
for their reorientation
before the birth process.

They must be
instructed about
all emergencies,
procedures, and
dangers.
They must also
be encouraged
to be daring.

Most of these animals
have had violent rejections
and painful experiences
with their owners
or with others,
and they may hesitate
or even reject
the idea of coming
into such contact
with humanity,
feeling
that such contact
will limit,
in a sense,
most of their freedom.

In the past
You very wisely established
rules and regulations
regarding marriage
and solved the problems
of sex.

But these animals
will start
with the ABC's
of these problems.

You must find
the ways and means
to protect
human beings
who are
centuries ahead of them
and not violate
Our code
of one humanity
and the rights
of each individual.

The First Ray Ashram,
of course,
has noticed many, many times
in the history
of the planet
that laws do protect,
but that laws also
prevent progress.

So each law
must be for
the Future —
but also meet
the needs of
the present.

I leave You
to plan these projects;
the full help
of all Ashrams
is needed.

Consider also
very thoroughly
the Law of Balance
in initiating
two lines of evolution
that are both extremes
but karmically
tied together.

As certain animals
incarnate,
another line of evolution —
the angelic kingdom —
will begin to incarnate
as humans.
They will have different
characteristics and
different goals.
At that time
You will be able
to train leaders

in such a way
that these threefold
evolutions — angels,
humans, and animals —
will proceed
in harmony,
in beauty.

In the past You built
the advanced esoteric
schools in many lands.
Now their graduates
must build collectively
the Sun Temple
with Seven Rays.
This temple will be
the source of
all knowledge
of the Seven Rays.

It will be built
upon a plateau
on a high mountain
surrounded by creeks,
deodars,
eucalyptus,
oak trees,

and all kinds
of flowers.

It will have
ten sections —
three for the three
departments of
the Hierarchy
and seven for
the seven Ashrams.

From this temple
will radiate
the wisdom
of the Sun.

Once a year
disciples
of various schools
will sit in conference
with the Heads
of the Ashrams.

> *Those who demonstrate*
> *the ability*
> *will be invited*

_to live in the University
of the Temple
and start their
superhuman evolution
toward Shamballa._

_The central room
on the seventh floor
will be dedicated
to the World Teacher._

_There will be
a great hall
for visitors from
our Solar System
and a contact point with
zodiacal fires._

_Our destination
will be to make
humanity
the World Disciple,
the Master
of the planet,
the Group Master._

The first two initiations
have been very successful.
The Third is spreading
a new, universal light
in all realms
of life.

The Fourth Initiation
will release
many prisoners of love —
Solar Angels —
for other
sacrificial responsibilities.

And You will not be surprised
if some advanced human beings
will want to serve
as Solar Angels
for newly incarnated
man
from the animal kingdom!

And the Fifth
will prepare humanity
for a greater
revelation.

In all of these
initiations,
all Ray Ashrams
will contribute
to prepare scientifically
correct ceremonies,
rituals, and sacraments
which will be used
in absolute privacy
by the Initiates.

The science of color,
of sound,
of movement,
of form,
and of great symphony
will be used.

Color,
sound,
movement,
and form
must be electrically
related to the Lives
and Guardians
of Fire.

*Through all this
the human soul
must be awakened
to higher responsibilities,
and a greater vision
in the Solar System,
the Zodiac,
and the Galaxy
will be revealed.*

> *Shamballa
> is always ready
> to give any assistance.*

*With this realization
We see that
the real function
of gratitude,
adoration,
and worship
is fusion with
a greater Reality
in the Cosmos
and a greater Freedom
in action.*

The last call
will be for
the preparation of
the Sixth Root Race.

As You are aware,
every great advance
is through destruction
of limitations.

> _This destruction_
> _is related to_
> _the form_
> _and is used_
> _as a means for_
> _a resurrection._

> _On all planes_
> _the Spirit_
> _will be set free_
> _in requisite degrees._
> _And this_
> _can be translated_
> _as great cataclysms_
> _on the planet._

We are close
to the culmination
of the seventh subrace
of the Fifth Root Race.

Already a few seeds
of the Sixth Root Race
are thrown
into the sphere
of Earth.

At the formation
of the fourth subrace
of the Sixth Root Race,
great cataclysms
will occur,
due to the accumulated karma
of past millenniums,
causing immense disaster.
And the Sixth Root Race
will be recognized
in its entirety.

The planet will have
a new map.
People will be

more etheric than physical,
and they will be androgynous.

The Eye which sees
past,
present,
and future
will function normally
in all men.

This Eye will be
the Eye that sees
reality,
which will be used
in full
intuitional awareness.

The future Sixth Root Race,
humanity in general,
will be
at the stage between
the Fourth and Fifth
Initiations.

And Those Who
can advance

a little farther
will be the seeds
of the future Seventh Root Race.

The future Races
will be planted
by the Masters
and Initiates,
and the children
must be protected
from any
negative influence.

My Warriors,
I will leave You
with these thoughts.

Fix Your eyes
upon the Future;
work diligently
for the needs
of the Future;
plan slowly,
wisely,
and with great
co-measurement.

There are now
millions and millions
of Sons of Light,
Sons of Love
and Power
ready to offer
Their lives
for this
great cause.

I bless You
with the blessings
of the Solar Lord
and call You
from refreshment
to labor.

When the Ancient of the Days —
the Lord of the World —
ended His words,
a huge rainbow sphere
surrounded the
great Assembly
of the Lords.

Seven great Angels
sounded Their seven notes
on Their golden conches,
creating a Cosmic Symphony.
The Taras in Their white robes stood up
in great reverence
as the Lord of the World
with His six Companions
and greater Presences
left the Council
and disappeared.

      And suddenly
      the whole assembly
      turned into a sphere
      of multicolored lights,
      in which I saw only
      palpitating stars.

Glossary

Agni Yoga: The Teaching that is given for this age and for the coming age is called the Teaching of fiery union, or in Sanskrit it is called Agni Yoga. Yoga means union. Agni means fire in its triple manifestation. This fire will create integration, alignment, at-one-ment in man, in humanity, in the solar system and the cosmos.

Ashram: Sanskrit word, refers to the gathering of disciples and aspirants which the Master collects for instruction. There are seven major Ashrams, each corresponding to one of the Rays, each forming groups or foci of energy.

Atmic vehicle: Body made of Atmic Plane substance.

Avatar: Great Being from solar or galactic fields sent cyclically to help humanity progress; they are condensed sources and embodiments of energy.

Buddhic vehicle: Body made of Intuitional Plane substance.

Center: Any energy vortex found in a human, planetary, or solar body; see also chakra.

Central Spiritual Sun: The Core of the solar system; the Sun is triple: the visible Sun, the Heart of the Sun, and the Central Spiritual Sun.

Chakra: Energy vortex found in each vehicle, relating to a particular part of the human body. There are seven primary chakras starting from the top of the head: (1) head, (2) throat, (3) heart, (4) solar plexus, (5) spleen, (6) sacral, (7) base of spine.

Chalice: See Lotus.

Cosmic Astral Plane: See Cosmic Planes.

Cosmic Magnet: The invisible center of the Universe.

Cosmic Mental Plane: See Cosmic Planes.

Cosmic Physical Plane: Refers to the lowest Cosmic Plane, consisting of the following planes: Divine, Monadic, Atmic, Intuitional or Buddhic, Mental, Emotional or Astral, and Physical. Each plane has seven subdivisions, totaling 49 planes of manifestation.

Cosmic Planes: The seven planes of Cosmic manifestation: Cosmic Physical, Cosmic Astral, Cosmic Mental, Cosmic Intuitional, Cosmic Atmic, Cosmic Monadic, and Cosmic Divine.

Deva: Belonging to the Angelic Kingdom, refers to beings following a different line of evolution than the human family.

Etheric body: The counterpart of the dense physical body, pervading and sustaining it. Formed by matter of the four etheric subplanes. The blueprint on which the physical body is based.

Great Invocation: A world prayer first published in 1945 by Alice A. Bailey.

Great Ones: Beings Who have taken the Fifth Initiation or beyond.

Hierarchy: The spiritual Hierarchy, Whose members have triumphed over matter and have complete control of the personality or lower self. Its members are known as Masters of Wisdom Who are custodians of the Plan for humanity and all kingdoms evolving within the sphere of Earth. It is the Hierarchy that translates the

Purpose of the Planetary Logos into a Plan for all kingdoms of the planet.

Higher Worlds: Those planes of existence that are of a finer vibration of matter than the physical plane. Generally refers to the higher mental plane and above.

Initiate: A person who has taken an initiation.

Karma, Law of: The Law of Cause and Effect or attraction and repulsion. "As you sow, so shall you reap."

Kumaras: Great Beings from other chains Who came to speed the evolution of our planet.

Lotus: Also known as the Chalice. Found in the second and third mental plane (from the top). Formed by twelve different petals of energy: three knowledge petals, three love petals, three sacrifice petals. The innermost three petals remain folded for ages. They are the dynamic sources of the nine outer petals. The Lotus contains the essence of all of a person's achievements, true knowledge, and service. It is the dwelling place of the Solar Angel.

Mahachohan: Also known as the Lord of Civilization.

Manu: A Great Being Who, at the first Round of the Earth Chain brought the archetypes of all future forms to earth. First Ray Lord.

Masters: Individuals Who had the privilege to master Their physical, emotional, mental, and intuitional bodies.

Mental body: The vehicle composed of the substance of the mental plane in which humanity expresses itself through thought.

Monad: Another term used to refer to the Core of the human being.

New Group of World Servers: Incoming New Age souls who work to manifest the Plan.

Plan: The formulation of the Purpose of the Planetary Logos into a workable program — a Plan — by the planetary Hierarchy for all kingdoms of Nature.

Purpose: That which the Solar Logos is intended to achieve at the end of the evolution of the solar system. The Plan is the formulation of this Purpose for our planet only.

Sanat Kumara: The physical incarnation of our Planetary Logos; He is the Lower Self, the Planetary Logos being the Higher Self; also called the Lord of the World, the Ancient of Days, the One Initiator.

Seven Rays: These are the seven primary Rays through which everything exists. They are pure energy, vibrating to a specific frequency and condensing from plane to plane, from manifestation to manifestation. The three primary Rays or Rays of Aspect are: The First Ray of Power, Will, and Purpose; The Second Ray of Love-Wisdom; The Third Ray of Active, Creative Intelligence. There are four Rays of Attribute: The Fourth Ray of Harmony through Conflict; The Fifth Ray of Concrete Science or Knowledge; The Sixth Ray of Idealism or Devotion; The Seventh Ray of Ceremonial Order and Finance. These Rays indicate qualities that pertain to the seven fields of human endeavor or expression.

Shamballa: Known as the White Island, it exists in etheric matter and is located in the Gobi desert. Shamballa is the dwelling place of the Lord of the World, Sanat Kumara, and is the place where "the Will of God is known."

Solar Angels: Very advanced Beings Who sacrificed Their life, descending from Higher Worlds to help the evolution of humanity and to guide its steps toward initiation. This happened on our planet at the middle of the Lemurian period. They are also called Guardian Angels, or Flames.

Soul: Also known as the Solar Angel.

soul: The small "s" soul is the human psyche, the Spark, traveling on the path of evolution having three powers: willpower, attraction, and intelligence to guide its development. Also known as the evolving human soul.

Synthesis, Law of: Synthesis is right relationship between units. It is the law that opens the path of infinite expansion and cooperation with all that exists.

Teaching, The: The sum total of the Teachings given by great Spiritual Teachers throughout time. Also referred to as the Ageless Wisdom, the Teaching, the Ancient Teaching.

Tower, The: See Shamballa.

Transfiguration: The result of the action of the electric fire of the Spiritual Triad on the higher mind. The lights in the little atoms of the personality vehicles are released, and the whole personality is purified in the Third Initiation.

Bibliographic References

Saraydarian, Torkom. Sedona, AZ: Aquarian Educational Group.

Legend of Shamballa, 1988.

Hierarchy and the Plan, 1992.

The Psyche and Psychism, 2 vols., 1981.

Saraydarian, Torkom. West Hills, CA: T.S.G. Publishing Foundation, Inc.

Other Worlds, 1991.

Index

path of, 67
world, 80
Universities
and end of war, 72
University, of Future
as Sun Temple, 183
Uranus, 17

V

Venus, 17
Vices
disappearance of, 22
See also individual listings
Vigilance, eternal, 159-160
Virtue, stage of
and use of machines, 115
Virtues, inner and powers
and value of man, 112
Vision, 8-9, 14, 17, 23, 25, 90,
99, 101, 171, 175, 188
etheric, 171

W

War, history of
and dealing with, 90
Waters of Life, 162
Weapons, eradication of, 7
White magic, 19-20, 23
Will, 9-12, 21, 42, 45-46, 55,
147-149, 154-159, 161, 163
defined for Future, 147, 155
Will
free, 10
loving, 163
of God, 10-12, 148
revelation of, 46

three qualities of, 154
Willpower, 28
energy of, 158
Women
emancipation of, 65
Work days
in Future, 164
Worship, 165, 188

Y

Year 1997-2025, 8
Year 2025, 7, 9
Year 2050, 16
Year 2075, 21
Year 2080, 22
Year 2085, 23
Year 2145, 24
Year 2200, 25
Year 2300, 25
Year 2400, 25
Year 2500, 25
Year 3000, 19
opening remarks, 32
Year 3000 & after
second objective / departure
of Buddha & Christ, 149
Third objective / Cosmic
evil, 155
Years 2025-2050, 13
Years 2030-2040, 12
Years 2045-2055, 15
Years 2600-2700, 25
Years 2700-3000, 25
Youth
now awakened, 82

About the Author

This is Torkom Saraydarian's latest published book. Many more will be released very soon. His vocal and instrumental compositions number in the hundreds and are being released.

The author's books have been used all over the world as sources of guidance and inspiration for true New Age living based on the teachings of the Ageless Wisdom. Some of the books have been translated into other languages, including German, Dutch, Danish, Portuguese, French, Spanish, Italian, Greek, Yugoslavian, and Swedish. He holds lectures and seminars in the United States as well as in other parts of the world.

Torkom Saraydarian's entire life has been a zealous effort to help people live healthy, joyous, and successful lives. He has spread this message of love and true vision tirelessly throughout his life.

From early boyhood the author learned first-hand from teachers of the Ageless Wisdom. He has studied widely in world religions and philosophies. He is in addition an accomplished pianist, violinist, and cellist and plays many other instruments as well. His books, lectures, seminars, and music are inspiring and offer a true insight into the beauty of the Ageless Wisdom.

Torkom Saraydarian's books and music speak to the hearts and minds of a humanity eager for positive change. His books, covering a large spectrum of human existence, are written in straightforward, unpretentious, clear, and often humorous fashion. His works draw on personal experiences, varied and rich. He offers insight and explanations to anyone interested in applying spiritual guidelines to everyday life. His no-nonense approach is practical, simple, and readily accessible to anyone who is interested in finding real meaning in life.

Torkom Saraydarian has de-mystified the mysteries of the Ageless Wisdom. He has made the much needed link between the spiritual and the everyday worlds.

Look for exciting new books, music, and videos being released by Torkom Saraydarian.

Other Books by
Torkom Saraydarian

The Ageless Wisdom
The Bhagavad Gita
Breakthrough to Higher Psychism
Challenge For Discipleship
Christ, The Avatar of Sacrificial Love
A Commentary on Psychic Energy
Cosmic Shocks
Cosmos in Man
Dialogue With Christ
Dynamics of Success
Flame of Beauty, Culture, Love, Joy
The Flame of the Heart
Hiawatha and the Great Peace
The Hidden Glory of the Inner Man
I Was
Joy and Healing
Legend of Shamballa
New Dimensions in Healing
Other Worlds
The Psyche and Psychism
The Psychology of Cooperation and Group
   Consciousness
The Purpose of Life
The Science of Becoming Oneself
The Science of Meditation
The Sense of Responsibility in Society
Sex, Family, and the Woman in Society
The Solar Angel

Spiritual Regeneration
Symphony of the Zodiac
Talks on Agni
Triangles of Fire
Unusual Court
Woman, Torch of the Future
The Year 2000 & After

Booklets

A Daily Discipline of Worship
Building Family Unity
Earthquakes and Disasters — What the Ageless
   Wisdom Tells Us
Fiery Carriage and Drugs
Five Great Mantrams of the New Age
Hierarchy and the Plan
Irritation — The Destructive Fire
The Psychology of Cooperation
Questioning Traveler and Karma
Responsibility
The Responsibility of Fathers
The Responsibility of Mothers
Spring of Prosperity
Synthesis
Torchbearers
What to Look for in the Heart of Your Partner

Video

The Seven Rays Interpreted

Next Book Release: **The Subconscious Mind
                    and the Chalice**

Ordering
Information

Write to the publisher for additional information regarding:

— Free catalog of author's books and music tapes

— Lecture tapes and videos

— Placement on mailing list

— New releases

Additional copies of *Olympus World Report...The Year 3000*

U.S. $18.00
Postage within U.S.A. $3.50
Plus applicable state sales tax

T.S.G. Publishing Foundation, Inc.
Visions for the Twenty-First Century
P.O. Box 4273
West Hills, California 91308
United States of America

Visions for the 21st Century®
P.O. Box 7068
Cave Creek, AZ 85331-7068 U.S.A.
Tel: (602) 502-1909
Fax: (602) 502-0713